Dr. Grace LaJoy Henderson

Foreword by **Pastor Dr. Donald D. Ford I**

AN URGENT CALL
TO THE *POWER* *of* MINISTRY

**REALIZING YOUR MINISTRY
THROUGH YOUR LIFE EXPERIENCES.**

Inspirations by Grace LaJoy
Raymore, MO 64083
www.gracelajoy.com
poetry@gracelajoy.com

An Urgent Call 	Dr. Grace LaJoy Henderson
To the Power of Ministry

The information in this book should not be used in lieu of, or take the place of, professional or Christian counseling.

The "gifts" that are referred to throughout this book are natural gifts and should not be confused with the spiritual gifts that are found in the Bible in Ephesians 4:11 and 1st Corinthians 12:7-10.

AN URGENT CALL TO THE *POWER* OF MINISTRY
Copyright ©2009-2011. Grace LaJoy Henderson.
Published by Inspirations by Grace LaJoy
Raymore, MO 64083
www.gracelajoy.com

Library of Congress Control Number: 2009922643

ISBN 978-0-9814607-6-5

All rights reserved. No portion of this book may be copied, reproduced or transmitted in any form without prior written permission from the publisher.

Printed in the United States of America

Praise for
AN URGENT CALL
TO THE *POWER* OF MINISTRY

"The impact of this book should stir you to action." – Pastor Dr. Donald D. Ford I – Touch of Grace Ministries of the Second Missionary Baptist Church, Grandview Missouri

"A must read book! Dr. Grace LaJoy engages the reader to examine their life and find out their true purpose. She has made it clear that the <u>power</u> of God is here for all who will receive Him into their lives." – Pastor G. Cornelius Jones, Author – Before You Marry Him: Six things he needs in his life

"This book is great for preachers, teachers and new church members. Pastors need a copy of this book for each of their members." – Christine T. White, Author – My Song

"Very well written, interesting and informative. When people read this book, they will find out that they have a greater purpose." – Minister Zenobia Smith, International Gospel Artist

"This book really helps people find what God has purposed them to do in their life. It is simple enough for new Christians to grasp. I would also recommend it to more mature Christians who are still wondering what their purpose is." – Minister James Lewis, New Life in Christ International Ministries

"As a pastor, this book caused me to reflect on how God used every one of my own experiences, good and bad, to lead me into ministry." – Pastor Rose Williams – Word of Deliverance Church

Praise continued...

I was greatly inspired by this book. It is written in such a clear way. It is going to help people. – A. Carr

"Very inspirational. I like the way Dr. Grace LaJoy teaches how God can use our life experiences to help reveal our ministry." – Tricia Piester, Speaker Trainer – Stonecroft Ministries

"Through Grace LaJoy's turbulent life story, I learned to never give up because God has a purpose for my life." – F. Island

"I most liked the author's life story. This is a great success story for people who may be going through a trial." – Lezlee Brown, Youth Leader

"An Urgent Call To The Power of Ministry gave me a greater awareness of my need to understand the words in the Bible." – C. Walker

"While reading An Urgent Call To The Power of Ministry, I was compelled to stop and ask, 'What is my gift?'. The insight shared by Dr. Grace LaJoy in this book helped me to recognize my gift!." – Arlivia White, Gospel Artist

"Anyone seeking to fulfill their purpose in life will benefit from this book." – Paula R. Thompson

Dedication

To my father, James Thompson, who passed away on March 8, 1990.

To my mother, Gloria Dawn Williams, who left me when I was two years old, never to return.

Acknowledgments

Aric J. Henderson, Arica N. Henderson, James D. Thompson, Gregory L. Thompson, Tyrone Thompson, Chrystal J. Thompson, Darlene L. Thompson-Williams, Paula R. Thompson, Sharon R. Thompson

An Urgent Call
To the Power of Ministry
　　　　　　　　　　　　　　Dr. Grace LaJoy Henderson

Table of Contents

Foreword	ix
Introduction	1
Preface	5
Chapter 1 - My Job is not my source - God Is	7
Chapter 2 - My Early Years	13
Chapter 3 - Signs of my Gift	23
Chapter 4 - Life Before Christ	29
Chapter 5 - My Personal Testimony	37
Chapter 6 - Life After Christ	47
Chapter 7 - Growing in my Gift	57
Chapter 8 - The Call to Minister	65
Chapter 9 - The Good News	73
Chapter 10 - The Power of Ministry	79
Closing - The Prayer of Salvation	87
Recommended books and resources	89
Glossary of terms	91
Index	93

An Urgent Call
To the Power of Ministry

Dr. Grace LaJoy Henderson

Foreword

We often are convinced that something needs to be done but are not always convicted that we are the ones to do it. We are often convinced that change or some ministry focus is needed to improve, impact and develop a greater awareness among our family, community and global relationships, but we are not convicted that we are the change agent who must discipline our lives to affect the lives of others.

<u>An Urgent Call to the Power of Ministry</u> taps into God's implication for all of us, who are indeed called according to His purpose. The Urgency has to do with the passion of the call. The Call itself is God making a specific call (selection) of a specific person for a specific purpose. The Power of the call comes from God's creative hand of placing the called (selected) one in various stages and platforms to act out, live out, and experience firsthand what God is doing with them to become the energy for what God will do through them in ministry to others.

Dr. Grace LaJoy Henderson clearly expresses what happens when one's relationship and life experience is deeply questioned, thoroughly searched, totally confronted, completely challenged, powerfully corrected, and spiritually changed by God's guiding hand. So much so, that you will want others to know and discover the empowering source of God's presence in and on their lives. The impact of this book should stir you to action.

Pastor Dr. Donald D. Ford I
Touch of Grace Ministries

> *"But you will receive power when the Holy Spirit comes on you; and you will be my witnesses in Jerusalem, and in all Judea and Samaria, and to the ends of the earth."*
> *Acts 1:8*
>
> *"He said to them, Go into all the world and preach the good news to all creation."* *Mark 16:15*

Introduction

"Publish!" "An Urgent Call to the Power of Ministry!" I heard as I slept comfortably in my bed during the middle of the night. I woke up partially, squirmed and returned to my sleep. Again I heard "publish!" I was so sleepy that I did not want to wake up. "An Urgent Call to the Power of Ministry!" I heard again. Finally, I realized that I would not be able to get back to sleep until I wrote these words down. The lights were off in my bedroom, so I felt around on the bookshelf on my bed until I found a pencil and a piece of a torn paper. I wrote down the words that I heard and finally, I was able to go back to sleep.

When I woke up later that morning, I remembered that I had written something down during the night, but I did not remember exactly what it was. So, I found the paper that I had wrote on, looked at it and saw the words, written in sloppy hand writing, "Publish, An Urgent Call to the Power of Ministry". Immediately, I knew that God had given me a title of a book that He wanted me to publish. There was only one problem…I knew nothing about being an author and furthermore, I knew nothing about that subject. In fact, the title did not make any sense to me. "Don't you mean

An Urgent Call to the *Ministry*"? I asked God. He answered, "No, I mean exactly what I said," "An Urgent Call to the *Power of* Ministry."

For years I struggled with that title because it just did not make sense to me. I had no idea what the content of the book was supposed to be. But, somehow I knew that if God told me to write it that He would eventually give me what He wanted it to be about. Several years went by before the title actually began to make sense to me. He did not reveal the entire meaning to me until I actually began writing the book about fifteen years later. He revealed to me that we need *power* to truly walk in ministry. He also revealed to me that it is vital that we realize this so our "ministry" work is not done in vain; So that souls would actually be saved as a result of our ministry; So that the good news of Jesus Christ can be spread as a result of our ministry.

God told me three things whenever I would begin to feel insecure about how I would write a book of this nature with my limited Christian experience. First, He told me that He will reveal to me what He wants the book to be about. Second, He told me that I would have the experience necessary to write the book by the time He was ready for me to write it. Third, He told me that when it was time for me to write the book, He would give me exactly what to write.

One of the major messages that God wants us to get from this book is the revelation of what *true* ministry is. There are <u>five</u> things that equal ministry: Preaching the Word of God, Teaching the Word of God, Sharing the Word of God, Sharing the good news of Jesus Christ, and sharing our testimony of salvation. (Mark 16:15)

In order to exercise *power* and be effective in ministry we must do several things: introduce listeners to the words that are in the Bible and not merely offer them a motivational speech; define Bible scriptures for the listeners without adding our own opinion; talk about the exact words from the Bible exactly as they are written, not adding or taking away from the scriptures; teach the listeners about Jesus; and let listeners know that they can have a relationship with God through Jesus Christ.

I used to think that the following things could be considered ministry: Working in a church auxiliary; inspirational and motivational speaking; and writing and publishing inspirational materials. But, I learned that while those "good works" are an important *part* of ministry, they do not *equal* true ministry. (Isaiah 64:6). Good works mean nothing unless the *power* is exercised in them.

The *power* that I am talking about is: God, Jesus, the Holy Spirit, and the words of the Bible. It is important that we understand the urgency of exercising the power in everything that we do in the name of ministry.

In this book, I share some of my turbulent life experiences. The purpose of sharing these experiences is to show you how God was preparing me for ministry from the beginning of my life; even from my mother's womb. (Psalm 139:13). It was the *power* of God on my life that helped me to overcome everything that I went through while growing up. It was those turbulent times that laid the strong foundation for me to share my testimony of God's power with others today.

So, it is urgent that we do not give up when we go through hard times in our lives. We can not afford to quit. It is urgent that we recognize the power of God in our lives and begin to share our testimony. It is urgent that we begin to share the good news of Jesus Christ. It is urgent that we understand that the *power* can not be found in our good works alone, but, in God, Jesus, the Holy Spirit, and the words in the Bible.

So, "An Urgent Call to the *Power* of Ministry" is defined as *"An important and a vital unction from God to share the good news of Jesus Christ"*.

Preface

The things that we go through in life are what prepares us for ministry. Both positive and negative experiences lead us to the purpose of ministry that God has for our lives. I am convinced that God does not allow us to go through things for no reason or just to hurt us; nor does he allow us to fall into sin and temptation to be judged by others or to suffer feelings of guilt and shame. Furthermore, God does not allow us to go through things so we can be embarrassed or hurt forever. But, so that we may fulfill our ministry by becoming a stronger person, and by sharing the good news of Jesus Christ with others.

Sometimes fear and shame hinders us from acknowledging our challenges, confessing our sins, and sharing our life experiences with others. When we keep it to ourselves, then it is impossible for others to be blessed, encouraged, empowered, uplifted, and delivered by the things that we have gone through.

Before I began writing this book, I often referred to my life experiences as my "testimony". But, as I was writing this book, God revealed to me that there was a difference between my "life experiences" and my "testimony". My life experiences are things that I have gone through in my life. But, my testimony is my personal account of the following things: How I came to know God; how I came to accept Jesus Christ as my personal savior; how I came to know that I am a part of God's family; how God delivered me from my sins; how I accepted God's forgiveness for my sins; and how my life changed after surrendering my whole heart to God.

Our life experience, however, may be shared *in conjunction with* our testimony, and it often is. But, the two have different definitions because sharing our *life experience* is different from sharing *Christ*. It is okay to share our life experience as long as we understand that our life experience alone is not our testimony if it does not reveal the truth of God's Word.

The positive thing about sharing our life experience is that it lets others know that they are not alone in their struggles, temptations, and imperfections. It is vital to share our testimony because two things happen when we share it: *We* get delivered and *others* get delivered. The Bible confirms that we overcome the works of Satan, God's enemy, by sharing our testimony (Revelation 12:11). When we hold back our testimony, we risk the possibility of never fulfilling our urgent call to the power of ministry!

Chapter 1
My Job is not My Source - God Is

I have had my share of unemployment. I have always been a good, dependable employee with a stable work history. I never got in any trouble on my jobs. However, I became unemployed one time because I hurt my hand during the initial training period and was unable to complete the training in the required time frame, and my ninety day probationary period was still in effect. I became unemployed another time due to the reorganization of the company; new administration came in and implemented new plans for my department that did not include me. I was offered a job in another department, but, I did not accept it and ended up unemployed.

While unemployed I began to think more seriously about writing full-time as opposed to a nine-to-five job. It was at that time that I officially founded my in-home publishing company by designing a website for the purpose of selling twenty laminated poetry posters, which featured poems I had written. It was at that time that I also began teaching myself how to do all of my own computer graphic design work. However, I quickly realized that it would be difficult to make money as a beginning writer so I went back to full-time employment only to become unemployed again.

Over the years, during my periods of unemployment, God blessed me with other forms of income that I did not expect. As a result, my children and I were never without the necessities of life and we did not want for anything either. I even purchased my first and second homes while working a seasonal job. God has always provided for the mortgage to be paid, I was never late on any bills, and my credit has always remained excellent.

When I knew I would soon be coming off my job, I began to think about, and was empowered by, the words of the leading motivational speaker, Les Brown. He stated if his job had not ended, he would not be a millionaire today. I felt my time was up at this job long before I actually left. I believed that when the time was right, God would allow me to come off my job and that when He did, it would not be grievous for me. I believed that the way would already be made for me; that He was in the process of preparing a pathway for me to follow; and that when I came off the job, all I would have to do is walk in the path that He had already set for me to follow. I strongly believed the bible verse that states, "all things work together for the good to them that love God, to them who are the called according to his purpose". (Romans 8:28).

While working full-time, before I left my job, I had began writing, producing, and publishing numerous inspirational books and resources. God revealed to me, during that time, that while the producing and publishing was good, the ultimate purpose for my life was to share information from the Bible, including the good news of Jesus Christ. The Bible confirmed that my job was to tell others about the power of Jesus and remind them of his commandments (Matthew 28:17-20). By that, I knew that God was calling me to understand His urgent call to the power of ministry. This enabled me to actually begin producing and publishing this book.

When I finally ended up off work and got the opportunity to concentrate on my writing full-time. It was at that time when I was given the opportunity to actually stand in front of groups of individuals, share my life experience, my testimony, and the good news of Jesus Christ. It was then that God revealed to me the full purpose of the inspirational books and other resources that I had worked so diligently to produce for so many years. These *products* were the things that would *finance* the actual ministry work that God called me to do.

Although my job is important, I have learned that my purpose is much bigger than my job. I see clearly that my job is not my source...God is. As I look back over my life, I can see that God began equipping me for ministry in my early years; and He has continued to prepare me for the day that I would be totally dependent upon Him as my source.

Chapter 1 - Discussion

My Job is not my Source - God Is

1. While unemployed, the author began to think more seriously about writing full-time, but, went back to a nine-to-five job when she realized it would be difficult to make money as a beginning writer.

   Is there something you desire to pursue in lieu of working on a nine-to-five job? If so, what is it that you desire to pursue?

2. The author's ultimate purpose is to share information from the Bible, including the good news of Jesus Christ.

   What do you think your ultimate purpose is?

An Urgent Call
To the Power of Ministry

Chapter 2

My Early Years

I was born an eight pound fourteen ounce baby girl in Kalamazoo Michigan, a small town just outside of Grand Rapids. According to my birth records, my father took me home from the hospital while my mother was unable to come home due to an extended illness at the time of my birth. I was the last of six children that my father and mother had together. As the baby of the family, I was affectionately called "Gracie" by my siblings.

"Your mother left, she doesn't want you" I was told at the age of two. My grandmother, who passed away in the year of 1991, would often fondly remember my cute, innocent reply, "well, if she don't want me, I don't want her needer!" However, my mother's leaving left me with feelings of fear and rejection. "If my own mother did not want me, then who else would want me?" I often thought. Today, when I think about the idea of an adult telling me that my mother did not want me, I think about what a horrible thing that was to say to a two-year-old child. I think about how devastating that must have been for me.

As I grew older, from the ages of two through six, I can remember school mates asking me, "Where is your mother?" I often found myself saying, "I don't have a mother." If they would inquire further about *why* I did not have a mother, I would reply, "none of your business!" Today, when I think about my reply, I realize that my response was a result of my feeling rejected by my mother. My classmates genuinely wanted to know and they did not mean any harm.

It was during this time that I can remember my first experience with writing poetry. I was in the first or second grade, and I remember taking the poem "roses are red, violets are blue, sugar is sweet and so are you" and changing it to say different words that I thought were more creative. Then I would proudly show other classmates, including my teacher what I had done with the poem. My gift of writing manifested itself at an early age, even though I did not recognize it as a gift. It was just something that I naturally enjoyed doing.

After my mother left, never to return, I lived with my father and my five siblings until I was seven years old. That was when my father took my oldest brother, who was fifteen years old at the time, to Florida with him; leaving me and my other four siblings in a house alone in Kansas City, Missouri. I was the youngest. The oldest child who was left in the house was my fourteen year old brother.

My father had asked a couple of people to check on us while he was gone. He had also promised to send us money for food and bills on a weekly basis. But somehow, the house that we were left in ended up with absolutely no food, no lights, no gas, no water, and no phone. Even the lock on the front door was broken off, leaving me feeling very afraid. I can remember my two brothers sleeping in shifts in front of the broken door in order to protect us from prowlers.

One morning at about two o'clock in the morning, I was awakened by a sheriff saying, "We are going to take you to an 'emergency foster home' for a nice hot breakfast." Those were the best words that I had heard in weeks! I did not hesitate to go with them...I was hungry! We finally pulled up in front of the emergency foster home. It was a small house, but, when we got inside the foster lady had cooked a large, hot breakfast in her very small kitchen. She had prepared eggs, bacon, sausage, grits, pancakes, toast...the works! She had gone out of her way to get up at two o'clock in the morning to cook all of that food just for us.

After we ate, we slept there for the night. A case worker picked us up the next morning to take us to a home that was supposed to be more permanent. I went on to live in three other foster homes. The conditions in the foster homes were sometimes horrid, scary, unfair, and unethical. However, the final foster home where I lived for three years actually offered me a stable home environment.

    Big Mama taught me how to cook, how to clean up, how to care for myself, including my hair, my body, my teeth, etc. She made sure we had a full breakfast, lunch and dinner everyday. We celebrated every holiday to the fullest. On Thanksgiving and Christmas she cooked mega-meals with all the trimmings. I usually got what I wanted for Christmas. Every Fourth of July, I got new clothes and we usually went to a park and had a big picnic. For Easter, I usually got new clothes and an Easter basket…and again Big Mama would cook a mega-meal. My foster father, Papa, would often take me to church so I usually went to church on Easter Sunday.

    Big Mama's home was the only home in which I ever remember having an adult to ensure that I got my homework done. I even got placed in the Gifted and Talented Program at the elementary school that I attended. However, I never felt like I was as smart as my classmates and I did not understand why the school chose me for the Gifted and Talented Program. It was not until later that I realized that God caused me to be gifted and talented and that He had been with me all along.

    While living with Big Mama, I saw my father again for the first time since he had left my siblings and me in that house alone. He came to the foster home to visit us. Big

An Urgent Call
To the Power of Ministry

Dr. Grace LaJoy Henderson

Mama offered him a seat in her very immaculate and clean living room. She told him how well we were all doing and how smart I was. He could see that we were living in a clean home and that we were well cared for. Before he left he gave me and my sister some money and promised to do all he could to prepare himself to bring us home with him. We were still living in Kansas City and he was living in North Carolina at that time. Both my foster mother and my case worker had always told me only good things about my father, so I could not wait for the day that he would finally get me out of the foster home and take me home to live with him.

When I was ten years old, the summer after I completed fifth grade, my father finally met all of the state requirements to be eligible to bring my siblings and me home to live with him. He sent bus tickets and my two sisters and I rode the bus from Kansas City, Missouri to Charlotte, North Carolina to be reunited with him and our three brothers. It was an extremely long twenty-three hour bus ride, but we finally reached the bus station in Charlotte, North Carolina where my father stood waiting for us to get off of the bus. The first place my father took us was to meet his girlfriend, Ms. Ruby, whom he had been in a relationship with for a number of years. Ms. Ruby was a woman with a small, petite stature and a cute, soft voice. She was very nice and treated me with love and respect from the first day that I met her. After meeting Ms. Ruby, my father took us to the three bedroom townhome where we would be living with him.

I started sixth grade in Charlotte, North Carolina, but before that year was over, we moved back to Kansas City, Missouri then to Detroit, Michigan. During the summer before I entered the seventh grade, we moved back to Charlotte, North Carolina, where my sister and I lived with my father and his girlfriend. By then, all of my other siblings had entered the military. From seventh grade until eighth grade my father moved us back and forth several times between Charlotte, Kansas City, and Detroit.

My most eventful times growing up was when I lived in Detroit. We always lived in the inner city area of the city so, I went to school with gangsters and students who carried guns and knives. It was challenging for me because I was always the "new kid" and so I had to work harder at building relationships with my school mates. I was not always accepted initially, but, it seems I would always meet at least one or two other children who were interested in being my friend. But, on the other hand, there always seemed to be someone at school who wanted to fight me for one reason or another.

God was my protection back then, for example, when I was "the new girl" at one neighborhood middle school in Detroit, there was a girl named "Tracy" who wanted to fight me. She admitted that I had not done anything to her, but that she was jealous because she felt that I was "taking all of her boyfriends". Just for the record, I was not interested in any of those guys but, as the "new girl", those guys found me attractive and desired to get to know me better.

Well, one day Tracy began telling people that she was going to beat me up after school. After school I was walking home with a friend, "Lisa" who had offered to help me fight if necessary. As Lisa and I were walking home we looked back and saw Tracy, but, she was not alone. There were gang members from a very popular all-girl gang walking behind her. I was nervous... "I can handle Tracy, I thought, but, I am afraid of those gang members". As the gang got closer and closer to Lisa and me, Lisa's father drove up in his car and took her away with him. Before they drove away, she asked her father if he could give me a ride home because I just lived right around the corner, but he was not willing to take me home.

Within seconds of Lisa leaving with her father, Tracy and the gang were in front of me ready for a fight. Tracy jumped in front of me prepared to fight; but before she and I could begin fighting, the leader of the gang that was with her jumped in front of Tracy and pushed her! To my surprise, the gang was following Tracy because they wanted to fight *her*, not help her fight *me*! When I look back on that experience as well as other similar experiences, I know without a doubt that God was protecting and preserving me for the purpose of ministry even in my early years.

Chapter 2 - Discussion

My Early Years

1. The author's first experience with writing poetry was in the first or second grade. She creatively changed the words to the poem, "Roses are red, Violets are blue…"

   Can you remember the first time you displayed a special talent? If so, what was the special talent and how did you display it?

Chapter 3
Signs of my Gift

After taking us back and forth with him from one state to another, eventually, my father made preparation for my sisters and me to live with an older lady in North Carolina while he continued his travels. However, he did prepare us, before he left, to care for ourselves. He armed us with information about how to support ourselves financially without him. "I'm not going to always be around" he would often say. He truly did all that he could to ensure that we would always be able to make it on our own. He was a man of wisdom.

At age thirteen, I began living with my eighteen year old sister. We lived in a townhome that charged rent according to our income. Since we did not have any income, we paid nothing for rent. I attended middle school and high school in North Carolina during the time period that we lived in the townhome. Those were some of my best and most memorable school years. For example, I had the opportunity to choose from various elective classes in high school. I chose classes like fashion merchandising, drama, acting, accounting and business. English and math were my favorite subjects.

I can remember a specific time, in eighth grade,

when my English teacher noticed my creative writing ability and gave me a compliment in front of the entire class. And since there was a boy in that class that I had a crush on, it made the teacher's compliment more meaningful to me. As part of the English curriculum, my teacher would often ask the students to write different types of stories. She would then read them, grade them, and return our papers to us.

Well, one day, after she had handed our papers back to us, she mentioned that there was one student in the class who wrote an exceptional story. That student was me! She went on to say that she loved to read all the stories that I wrote because she always looked forward to finding out how my creative stories would end. That really made me feel good, but, I still did not recognize that writing was my gift.

I was thirteen years old, in the ninth grade, when I kept my first poem. It was a poem about a boy that I liked; I even set the poem to music and sang it as a song. When my sister read that poem about the boy that I liked, she told me that I had a special talent and that everyone could not write poems the way that I did. She often told me that I had a gift to write. From that time on, I began to share my poetry, songs, raps and stories with friends and family who usually asked if they could have a copy of my writing. "I can not give you a copy because I am going to write a book one day", I would always say. I can recall another time, in high

An Urgent Call Dr. Grace LaJoy Henderson
To the Power of Ministry

school, when my acting teacher recognized my creative talent and shared her kind thoughts about me and my work with all of the students in the class. But, I still did not recognize my gift at that time.

It was difficult for me to recognize that I could have any type of a gift when I spent most of my early years thinking I was "hard-headed". As I was growing up and living with my father, he often told me I was "hard-headed" when I misbehaved. The interesting part about it was that I actually believed him! It was during my high school years in North Carolina that I first realized that I was not "hard-headed". Here is how I came to that realization:

I was sent to the principal's office because I had disobeyed the schools behavior policy. The principal noticed something special about me. He informed me that I had decent grades and that I seem to have a lot of friends, so he did not understand why I had disobeyed. When he asked me why I disobeyed, I responded, "it is because I am hard-headed". After I said that, I noticed that the principal was looking at me with disbelief. So, to convince him I said, "really, I am hard-headed, that is what my daddy has always told me, so that is why I have always disobeyed". The principal looked at me with compassion in his eyes and said, "no, you are not hard-headed", and I actually believed him! So, from that day on, I knew that I was not "hard-headed".

Signs of my Gift

I believe that my daddy had good intentions and that he would never have purposely said anything to me that he knew would negatively affect my self-esteem. But, I thank God for using the principal, as well as other people throughout my life, to empower me and to help me realize that I am special. My English teacher, acting teacher, sister, and friends all noticed my writing creativity, but I still did not recognize the signs of my writing gift.

Chapter 3 - Discussion

Signs of my Gift

1. One of the author's favorite subjects in middle and high school was English and eventually she realized that she had a gift of writing.

    What is/was your favorite subject(s) in middle and high school?

    Do you think your favorite subject(s) is an indication of your gift? Why or why not?

2. Even though signs were present, the author was not aware that she had a gift to write.

    Can you think of some signs that may indicate what your gift could be? If so, what are the signs?

    Name one or more people who have noticed something special about you? What exactly did they notice about you? Do you think that what they noticed could be your gift? Why or why not?

Chapter 4
Life Before Christ

God spared my life when I was thirteen years old. Here is how it happened: It was after one o'clock in the morning, and I was walking home from a YMCA dance party with "Ron" a fifteen year old boy. Ron was not my boyfriend or anything like that, he had just offered to walk home with me because I did not have a ride and we both lived in the same townhome complex. Initially, as we were walking home, I was walking on the outside of the road, which did not have a sidewalk. Suddenly, a car drove past really fast, so Ron offered to take the outside of the road so that I could be safe. Then, the next car that drove by hit him and sped away! Ron did not survive. If I had stayed on the outside of the road, then it would have been me that got hit instead of him. I believe that God spared my life on that North Carolina road for a reason...so that I could one day walk in the power of the ministry in which He called me.

When I was sixteen years old, I had to leave North Carolina abruptly to move to Kansas City. It was the summer after I completed the eleventh grade. I really liked living in North Carolina and had made a lot of good friends over the years that I lived there, especially during my high school years. For example, I had a good friend named Nena who I often spent time with over a period of about five years. I left North Carolina so abruptly that I did not get to say goodbye to her and lost touch with her. We reunited after twenty years and she often reminds me of how I used to make up funny raps and creatively change words to popular songs in a way that made her laugh. She had no idea that my silly actions back then would result in such a powerful writing gift twenty years later!

As hard as it was to leave North Carolina, I eventually got accustomed to living in Kansas City again during my senior year in high school. I met a lot of new friends and even won homecoming queen! I also found myself exercising my poetic skills during my senior year. For example, I entered two poems into a poetry contest and one of them won third place and the other one received an honorable mention. This was also the year that I wrote the most poems about boys. Some of the poems did not portray good morals, but they did portray the truth about what many young girls my age were experiencing with boys during that era. By the middle of my senior year, I had a collection of poems.

One day, I unknowingly left my collection of poems in my home economics classroom. I realized I had left them when I was sitting in my economics class one day. My teacher held the stack of poems in her hand as she asked "who wrote this poem about 'Life'?" When I told her that those were my poems, she looked at me with a proud smile on her face and said, "you *do* have talent, don't you?" That made me feel very encouraged, but I still did not realize that writing was my gift. During the last days of my senior year, leading up to graduation, several of my teachers wished me luck with my writing even though writing was not one of my future goals. I worked for a fast-food restaurant immediately after high school graduation. Even though my senior high school teachers recognized my writing gift, I did not. My after graduation goal was to become more efficient on a computer word processor and maybe become a secretary.

During the summer after I graduated from high school at age seventeen, I had sex for the first time and got pregnant out of wedlock. So, I was pregnant when I began to attend a local community college in the fall of 1984. I had to drop out of college when I was eighteen years old to give birth to my beautiful baby girl who I named Arica Nicole. But, I returned to college afterwards long enough to earn a clerical science certificate. By the time I gave birth to Arica at age eighteen, I had moved out of my sister's apartment and had begun living in an apartment on my own. God was truly with me after I had Arica. For example, Arica's grandmother (her father's mother) offered to be there for me. She told me that if I needed *anything* that I could ask her for it and she would provide it for me. "If you can name it, you can claim it!" she assured me. She kept every promise that she made to be there and provide for me. I know that I could not have made it without her help.

She was at the hospital with me during my very hard delivery. After I was released from the hospital, I could barely walk. So, she took me into her home and took care of me. She did everything from preparing my baby's bottles to cooking and serving me breakfast, lunch, and dinner daily until my body was healed and I was able to care for myself and my baby. After I regained my strength, I took Arica and went back to the apartment that I was renting.

Although I had moved into the apartment while I was pregnant, I had not really lived in it because I had gone back to stay with my sister until I gave birth. So, on my first night in the apartment with my new baby, I discovered that it was infested with mice. I have always been afraid of mice, and I certainly did not want my baby living in this type of environment. So, on that night, I left the apartment with my baby and ended up living with my baby's aunt "Peaches" (Arica's father's older sister), who took care of me until I found another apartment to live in.

I finally found another apartment, but during my first night in the new place, I heard a lot of loud talking and cussing going on outside. And on the first morning that I woke up in the new apartment, I heard a couple of men outside of my front door gambling with dice and cussing. I quickly realized that I was living in an unsafe, drug infested environment with my new baby. This made me feel scared, but I did not move out. I just prayed and asked God to bless me with a clean, quiet, safe place to live as soon as possible.

It took six months, but, God finally answered my prayer when he allowed an apartment manager to show me favor. She had informed me that there was a two year waiting list and that the apartment complex generally only catered to low-income individuals who were retired and had no children. But, she made an exception and allowed me to move in after being on the waiting list for only six months. I moved into the apartment with my seven month old daughter and lived there for seven years. During that time I began working seasonal for the federal government, got married, had a second child named Aric Jamal, got divorced, and went back to college. But most importantly, during that time, I gave my life to God.

My first introduction to God was actually from my mother, when I was just a baby, before she left. Although I was only around the age of one, I remember being in church and seeing my mother playing the piano in the pulpit area. I also remember when she would proudly ask me, in the presence of the church daycare workers, "where is God?"

and I would point my finger up to the sky. Then she would say, "Where is the devil?" and I would point my finger down to the ground. Then she would give me a hug and be so proud of me. But even though my mother taught me about God at a young age, I still needed to know him for myself. As I grew up, without a mother, I went to church at every opportunity. But, I was still a sinner who needed to surrender my life to God.

So, during this very volatile period, God spared my life. He allowed others to notice my writing gift. He was with me as I began my adult life as a single parent and truly provided for me during my life before Christ.

Chapter 4 - Discussion

Life Before Christ

1. The author feels that God spared her life so that she could one day walk in the power of ministry.

   Can you think of a time when God spared your life? If so, what was the situation? For what reason do you feel he spared your life?

2. The author's friend Nena fondly remembered when the author used to make up funny raps and creatively change words to popular songs.

   Is there something about you that stands out to your friends? If so, what is it?

3. The author's mother is the one who first introduced her to God.

   Do you remember the first time you heard about God? If so, who told you about Him and what did they say about Him?

An Urgent Call Dr. Grace LaJoy Henderson
To the Power of Ministry

Chapter 5

My Personal Testimony

As a result of my father moving me from one state to another, I ended up going to several different denominations of churches. Whenever we moved to a new place, I would walk to the nearest church in my neighborhood. It did not matter to me what denomination the church was, I just wanted to go to church. I noticed some differences in the churches that I attended. For example, one church may sing a song very slowly with a soothing melody, while another church may sing the exact same song very fast with an upbeat melody.

However, I found *one* common thing in all of the churches: The *power* of the Holy Spirit! I always felt uplifted after every service regardless of the church's denomination. From this experience, I learned to respect and appreciate different church denominations. As long as they preached about God's Word and shared the good news of Jesus Christ I was satisfied. A person's denomination is not as important as their personal relationship with God.

For years, before I actually developed a personal relationship God, I thought I had already done it for the following reasons: I went to church every Sunday; I did not engage in a lot of the sinful actions that other people engaged in; I asked Him to come into my life when I was twelve years old; I got baptized when I was sixteen; I asked Him to come into my life again when I was eighteen; I did not know that there was more to giving my life to God. Being in church, I had heard a lot about the Holy Spirit, the power of God, His unspeakable joy, and the peace of God that surpasses all understanding. But, I had not experienced it. Furthermore, I did not realize that I had not experienced it.

Over the years many people told me about God's son, Jesus Christ and His love for me and tried to get me to truly accept Him (2 Thessalonians 2:16). For example, I began going to night clubs at age twenty-three and I was getting ready to go out one night when I received a call from a friend. Yvonne informed me that God told her to call me to tell me the good news of Jesus Christ; How I could receive God's forgiveness for my sins and have eternal life through Jesus Christ (Romans 6:23).

When Yvonne informed me of this, two thoughts overwhelmed me: First of all, I thought I had already given my life to God. So, I resented her because I felt that she was indicating that she was better than me or that she knew more about God than I did. Second of all, I was really looking forward to going to the night club and I knew in my heart that if I accepted what she was telling me that I would not be able to go out that night. So, I convinced Yvonne that I

An Urgent Call To the Power of Ministry

Dr. Grace LaJoy Henderson

knew just as much about God as she did and that she was wrong for calling me trying to act like she was better than me. After trying to convince me to accept God's forgiveness for over an hour, she finally gave up and apologized, so I was free to go to the night club.

About one month later, I accepted God's forgiveness. Yvonne was the first person that I called to tell about it. I was finally able to tell her that, on that night when she called to tell me about Jesus, *everything* she said was right and *everything* that I said was wrong. I had been unable to receive God's forgiveness because I thought I already had it, and I did not think I was a sinner. So, my heart had not been open to receive it.

But, it was a lady at work who finally helped me understand my own personal need for God's forgiveness, when I was twenty-six years old. Gloria sat next to me at work and she recognized that I knew a lot about God. But, she also recognized that I had not allowed Him to truly come into my heart and control my life. I would tell her about my church experiences as well as my night club experiences. When she talked about God I talked with her because I felt that I knew him just as well as she did. After all, I went to church every Sunday.

One day, as I was sharing my spiritual knowledge with Gloria, she told me that I had not accepted God's forgiveness for my sin; therefore, I did not have eternal life. I did not feel that she had the right to judge whether or not I had eternal life, but she told me that she had the right to judge me according to God's Word. She told me about the section in the Bible that states, "you will know them by their fruit" (Matthew 7:20). She saw no fruit or evidence that I had a personal relationship with God.

She told me that she could tell that I really *wanted* to have a personal relationship with God, but unfortunately she said I did not have it yet. I wanted her to take those words back and agree that I did. I *needed* her to agree that I knew God as well as she did or else I could not move on. She refused to take her words back and she would not agree with me. So, I began to ask her questions about why she felt that I did not have a personal relationship with God.

I began to ask her for explanations about different sections from the Bible that I had heard all of my life. She took the time to explain what each one meant and patiently answered every question that I had. Then she began offering me more sections from the Bible to read. Even though I had heard these words in church all of my life, she told me that I needed to actually read them in the Bible for myself. So, I went home that Tuesday, pulled my Bible out, dusted it off and began reading the sections of the Bible that Gloria had given me. And for the first time in my life each and every word of the Bible readings actually made sense to me!

One section of the Bible, in particular, that made sense to me was the section that talks about how many will stand in front of God and say, "Lord, I have done many wonderful things for you". But, He will say to them "go away from me, I never knew you". (Matthew 7:23). From that I realized that even though I thought I was basically a good person; and even though my friends often complimented me on what a good person I was, I did not know God. I realized that my good works meant nothing to God because it was my *heart* that he wanted. Another section of the Bible that made sense to me was the section that says, "Trust in the Lord with all of your heart and do not depend on your own understanding." (Proverbs 3:5). From this, I realized that I had been trying to do good by myself, without the help of God.

I came back to work on Wednesday and reported to Gloria how much I actually understood the Bible readings that she had given me. So, she gave me some *more* sections of the Bible to read. She told me that the Bible is God's Word. (John 1:1). She informed me that the absolute *only* way to get to know God and develop a relationship with Him is to read the Bible for myself. "It is *God's Word* that is going to cause you to have a personal relationship with Him", she said.

I continued to read the different sections of the Bible that she gave me to read and by that Friday morning, I had totally received the revelation of God's Word in my heart and accepted His forgiveness for my sins! Many people have argued that Gloria should not have told me that I did not have eternal life, but, that is what it took for me to get it. I needed someone who would be real with me and tell me the truth and to not back down when I insisted on being right; and not apologize to me for offending me after telling me the truth. If Gloria would not have stood her ground with me, I would not have accepted God when I did; and I do not know if or when I would have had another opportunity to give my heart to God.

After I gave my heart to God and He revealed His Word to me, Gloria explained to me the power of the Holy Spirit. She explained that the Holy Spirit is the spirit of God, which lived in His son, Jesus Christ. So, when God sent Jesus Christ to die on the cross for our sins, He left His Spirit. She also explained to me that God, Jesus Christ, and the Holy Spirit are all one person. She assured me that the Holy Spirit would…

…never leave me nor forsake me. (Hebrews 13:5)
…keep me from turning back to my sinful lifestyle. (Jude 1:24)
…help me grow in my relationship with God. (Ephesians 4:13-15)
…teach me everything that I need to know. (John 14:26)

An Urgent Call 　　　　　　Dr. Grace LaJoy Henderson
To the Power of Ministry

...remind me of the teachings of Jesus. (John 14:26)

...give me comfort (John 14:6)

...be my helper. (Acts 10:38)

...lead, guide, and direct me. (Psalm 73:24)

...be my strength and power. (Acts 1:8)

...give me peace and joy. (Romans 14:17)

...give me everlasting life! (Romans 6:22)

    I am confident that I am a new person because of Jesus Christ. (2 Corinthians 5:17). I am confident that the Spirit of God is living on the inside of me, giving me comfort, and teaching me everything that I need to know to continue my walk with God. (John 14:26).

    Other people's experience of how they developed a personal relationship with God may be different from mine. But, every personal testimony has <u>one</u> thing in common: The *power* of God. It is the power of God that gives everlasting life to everyone who believes the good news of Jesus Christ. (Romans 1:16). I am convinced that God does not care what church denomination we are a part of. However, He does want us to have a personal relationship with Him through His Son, Jesus Christ. (John 14:6).

My Personal Testimony

Chapter 5 - Discussion

My Personal Testimony

1. The author credits Gloria for causing her to accept the good news of Jesus Christ.

   Do you have a personal relationship with God?

   If so, who do you credit for telling you the good news about Jesus Christ?

   If not, has anyone ever talked to you about God's forgiveness?

   If someone has ever talked to you about God's forgiveness, who was it? What exactly did they tell you about it?

2. Gloria recognized that the author needed a personal relationship with God and told her that the Bible was the only way to develop the relationship.

   Do you read the Bible? If so, how often do you read it? If not, why not?

   If you read the Bible, describe how reading it has helped you.

Chapter 6
Life After Christ

Many things happened after I gave my life to God. I began to actively work in the church, I realized that writing was my gift, and both of my children developed their own personal relationship with God. I believed in staying busy in the church as the Bible says, "do whatsoever your hands findeth to do." (Ecclesiastes 9:10). As a result of that belief, I worked with children for over ten years as a children's church and youth worker, Sunday school teacher, vacation bible school teacher and youth drama department director. In addition, I worked in the church kitchen and as the assistant editor of the church newsletter. I also assisted in many other areas of ministry as needed.

As youth worker, I got the opportunity to produce and direct a play that I had written entitled, One Woman's Testimony, a play that portrayed how I came to accept God's forgiveness of my sin. I still did not realize that I had a writing gift at that time, but, I enjoyed the opportunity to share my testimony, in a creative way, with other church members.

While working as youth drama department director, God revealed some things to me about the writing gift that He had given me. During this time I got the opportunity to produce and direct two more plays that I had written, entitled In My Mama's House and God Will Make A Way. Before the production of In My Mama's House, God had given me numerous songs, as I slept, over a period of several years. Whenever He would give me a song in my sleep, I would wake up and use my voice to record the words, melody, and the music on a tape recorder that I kept beside my bed.

For years, I did not understand why He gave me songs when I did not sing or play an instrument. But I realized, during the production of this play, that about four of the songs that I had written went perfectly with the play. This was the very first time that God gave me a clue about what He wanted me to do with some of the songs that He had given me. Four more of the songs were used during the production of the play, God Will Make A Way.

I can remember the day that God revealed to me that writing was my gift. I was off work on that day and I found myself talking to God about His purpose for my life. For months I had been asking God, "What is my gift?" Even though he had already given me several hints: I had been writing poetry and songs for over ten years at that time; I had tablets and boxes full of poetry and stage plays that I had written; I had cassette tapes full of songs that often came to me as I slept; People often complimented me on my writing skills. But, even with those hints, I continued to ask, "God, what is my gift?"

Well, on this particular afternoon, I went to the park to take a walk and while I was walking God revealed to me that I was a writer. Not only did I write poems, songs and plays, I also kept a written journal of my dreams. God revealed to me that writers write; that is what they do; writers are called writers because they write. So, from that day on, it was clear to me that the gift that I had been asking God to show me was actually the thing that I enjoyed doing the most.

After I knew what my gift was, my next challenge was to figure out what to do with it. I did not know where to begin or who to ask. The people who I attempted to get answers from either did not know or were not willing to share their information with me. So, it was several years between realizing my gift and actually writing my first book. But, in the meantime, I continued to write poems and songs until one day God spoke to me and said, "now it is time to do something with what I have given you". It was at that point that I created five laminated posters from five of my favorite poems that I had written. I began selling them and giving them away.

My church family began to recognize that I could write poetry and often asked me to write and read poems for special events. I eventually became the go-to person

An Urgent Call To the Power of Ministry

whenever a poem was needed to appreciate and honor deserving individuals in the church. At first, when my church family began asking me to write poems, I would agree to write it as long as someone else would read it. But, eventually I began to realize that it was an honor to be able to read the poem that I wrote, so I started reading them as well. As I continued to write and read poems for the church congregation I began to receive a lot of compliments on my work. "That was a beautiful poem, you are so talented!" people would often say. For a long time I thought they were just being nice, but, after about five years of compliments I realized that everyone could not be just lying to me.

After realizing that there must be some truth to the compliments, I began to have more confidence in the gift of writing that God had given me. I had always known that my writing was meant to bless millions of people, but, the compliments were a great encouragement to me. Soon after my confidence began to be build, I began working on my first book of Christian poetry. I was working in several church auxiliaries at that time and began to drop out of them one-by-one, slowly but surely. The more I began to produce and promote my writing, the more I had to let go of the things that I was doing in the church. I believed that my writing was the ministry that God had called me to do.

Between working in the church and realizing my

writing gift, I continued to raise my two children as a single parent. I began taking them to church when they were babies and I often watched as they walked up to the altar during the altar call. I saw them crying out to God and I knew that they both really wanted to give their whole hearts to God. As they were growing up, I often asked God to allow my children to develop their own personal relationship with Him before they went off to college. God answered my prayer! Both of my children accepted God's forgiveness for their sins before they went off to college.

There was a time when I did not foresee my children attending college for two reasons: I had never attended a four-year college and only had a one-year certificate in Clerical Science; I did not have the finances for my children to attend college. But, when I was twenty-six years old I got the opportunity to return to college. I remember the day that I received the good news. Although I had desired to return to college, I had defaulted on a student loan and was not eligible for federal student financial aid and could not afford to finance my own college education.

I had gotten laid off from my seasonal job and went to the unemployment office to try to find a job. Although I went there to find a job, the unemployment specialist who was assisting me ended up telling me about a program that would pay for me to go back to college. The program was specifically for people like me who were not eligible for federal student financial aid. I accepted the information, returned to college, and completed an associate's degree in Office Management.

While I am on the subject about the unemployment specialist who assisted me, I am reminded of something else: Without knowing anything about me she saw something special in me and told me that I could be the next Maya Angelou. She was not even aware that I wrote poems! She also told me that she would like it if I could speak to a group of girls that she worked with in her spare time. She thought that I would be the perfect person to speak to her group. At that time, however, I could not imagine myself speaking to a group of any kind. I felt very afraid about the possibility of speaking to her group of girls, but, I never heard from her after I left the unemployment office that day so I felt relieved!

Well, after I completed my associate's degree, I continued going to college until I earned a bachelor's degree in Social Psychology. Through a series of events, I earned a master's degree and a PhD in Christian Counseling with an emphasis in writing and research. Even the chairman of the Bible college that I attended noticed something special about me. I had completed one poetry book entitled, More Than Mere Words: Poetry That Ministers when I was seeking admittance into the college. I presented the book to the chairman to see if I could possibly receive college credit for having written the book.

Not only did I receive college credit, but when the chairman found out that I had published my poetry book myself, he challenged me to build a course that would teach students of the college the steps necessary to publish their own books. I accepted the challenge, built the course, and taught it to a group of students as a sixteen week class that next semester. When I graduated with my master's degree and PhD, my children attended my graduation and were very proud of me.

After completing college, I actually began to see the possibility of my children going off to college after they graduated from high school. I believe that my diligence in going back to college empowered my children to know that they could do it too. As time went on, I began to do everything in my power to ensure that my children's education would be financed and that nothing would stop them from attending college. Between federal financial aid and academic scholarships, both of my children ended up going to college.

So, I experienced a lot of great things after accepting God's forgiveness and receiving the Holy Spirit. Not only did God bless *me*, He blessed both of my children as well.

He blessed them naturally and spiritually, and it was all a Result of the one decision that I made to give my life to God.

Chapter 6 - Discussion

Life After Christ

1. After the author gave her life to God, she began working in the church, she realized her gift of writing and both of her children developed their own personal relationship with God.

   Name some things that have happened to you since you gave your life to God.

   Name one or more people who have given their life to God as a result of your commitment to God.

   If you have not given your life to God at this point, what things would you like to have happen in your life? In someone else's life?

2. At one point the author had been writing poetry and songs for over ten years, and even had tablets full of poetry, songs and stage plays. But, she still did not know what her gift was.

   Can you think of something that you have enjoyed doing in your spare time. If so, what is it? Do you think that it could be your gift? Why or Why not?

3. True or False: The gift that God revealed to the author was actually the thing that she enjoyed doing the most.

Chapter 7

Growing in my Gift

After I completed my PhD, I took the material that I used to teach the book publishing course, edited it, and published it in a book entitled, Writer's Breakthrough: Steps to Copyright and Publish Your Own Book. This book offers writers and aspiring authors step-by-step instructions about how to publish their own book. Writer's Breakthrough was the second book that I published. The title of my very first book was More Than Mere Words: Poetry That Ministers.

I can remember knowing, as I was putting the book together, that some people could possibly be critical of my work or judge me by what I wrote, but, I knew that I could not let that stop me. My goal for publishing the book was for it to reach the people who God wanted it to reach; the people who would ultimately be blessed, empowered, and inspired by the book. Knowing that each and every poem in the book would inspire somebody is what motivated me to keep moving.

After I completed the publishing of More Than Mere Words: Poetry That Ministers, my pastor at the time, Bishop Mark C. Tolbert, was gracious enough to allow me to have my first book signing after one of our church services. He also allowed me to read poetry to the congregation, during the church service, on that day. It turned out that the leading motivational speaker, Les Brown, would be the guest speaker at our church on that same day. Mr. Brown was sitting in a chair in the pulpit area when I read a poem from my poetry book entitled, I Forgive You. So, when it was his turn to speak, he told the congregation that the words of that poem meant a lot to him. Then he proceeded to tell the entire story of why that poem meant so much to him. He also interjected some good words about me and my poetry book while he was speaking.

After the Sunday service was over I was selling and autographing books at my table and Mr. Brown's product sales table was set up right beside mine. Between product sales and autographs, I asked Mr. Brown if I could take a picture with him and he said "sure". Then he requested to hold a copy of my poetry book and said, "I want to endorse you". So, he held my book and we took a picture together.

People often ask me how I got an endorsement from this great motivational speaker. From this experience, I learned that when I begin to do what God has given me to do, then God will take care of everything else. He will even supply the *endorsements* that I will need as I proceed to the next level in my gifts, talents, and most of all, in my ministry.

Realizing that there were other writers who had a

An Urgent Call To the Power of Ministry — Dr. Grace LaJoy Henderson

God-given gift to write, who may not know where to begin in sharing their gift with others, I had developed a two-page outline which contained the steps that I took to publish my own book. I gave the outline away during my first book signing to those who asked me how I got my book published. I eventually expanded the information from the outline and it became the Writer's Breakthrough book that I spoke about earlier.

After publishing my first two books, I began receiving more invitations to read poetry and conduct workshops for writers at churches, libraries, conferences and other community events. I also designed, and began conducting, a special annual Writer's Breakthrough Workshop.

Between reading poetry, speaking, and conducting writer's workshops, I knew that I had more unfinished books sitting on my book shelf that would eventually need to be published. So my next project was to publish my Poetic Book Series. I created the series by taking five of my poems, adding illustrations to them, and making them into five small books. One of the books from the Poetic Book Series, entitled Diversity in our Schools, was adopted by a local school district. The school district uses the book as part of their diversity education program for their second graders.

After publishing the Poetic Book Series, there were

still four more books sitting on my bookshelf that needed to be published. But I had become very busy during that time, so I suspected that it would be at least another five years before I would actually have the time to publish any more books. But, to my surprise God spoke to me sooner than I could ever have imagined and told me that those books had no business sitting on my bookshelf. He instructed me to publish them immediately! Then He supplied me with *everything* that I needed to do it: the time, the patience, the motivation, the energy, the discipline, the finances and *all* of the other resources.

    I began publishing these books and within one year they were all released. The titles of the four books were Sexual Purity and the Young Woman, Understanding Each Other, In My Mama's House, and How Can Jesus Be God. There is a story behind why I wrote each of these books. For example, with the sexual purity book, I was asked to teach a group of girls during a woman's workshop at the church that I was attending. I developed an outline of my lesson and wrote out my presentation. When I presented the information to the girls, I was impressed with how eager the girls were to open up and talk about their experiences with opposite sex relationships. By this, I realized this subject needed to be introduced to more young girls. So, I put the outline and presentation on my bookshelf with the intention of one day writing a book entitled, Sex and Teen Girls. It was about twelve years from the time I taught the girls until the book was actually published.

When it was finally time to publish the book, I felt that there was something missing. So, I decided I would start writing a new book from scratch and entitle it, Sexual Purity and the Young Woman. I designed a set of questions about sexual purity and asked my daughter to answer each of them. After reviewing her responses, it dawned on me that everything she wrote in response to the questions would make a great introduction to the Sex and Teen Girls book.

So, I took the Sex and Teen Girls book off of the book shelf, removed the introduction that I had in it and replaced it with the information that my daughter had written. Then I renamed the book from Sex and teen Girls, to Sexual Purity and the Young Woman, a reference guide for teen and college aged girls. I asked my daughter to review, edit, and add her input to the book. I also asked her to assist me with defining key words for the back of the book. Her input was significant enough for me to name her as co-author of the book. There are similar stories of how all of my books came to be published.

While I was publishing those four books, I was also producing my first spoken word poetry CD, Poetic

Empowerment. The CD features myself reading poems that I wrote with music that fits the rhythm and message of the poems on the CD. In addition to publishing all of my own books, I have also assisted other writers in realizing their dream of becoming an author. For example, Christine T. White became a new author, at eighty plus years old, when I assisted her with writing and publishing her autobiography.

I met Mrs. White at a church event and she told me she had desired to publish her autobiography for several years. She wanted to leave family history for her nieces, nephews, family and friends. For about four weeks, Mrs. White talked about her life while I listened and wrote her story. Within two months she was the proud author of her first book entitled, My Song.

I have learned that whenever God gives me something to do, He does the work through me and supplies everything I need to do it. He supplies the confidence, motivation, energy, finances, volunteers, etc. He even gives me stamina and endurance to complete the projects that I start. More importantly, He sends other people to me who need the resources that he has so graciously given to me, allowing me the opportunity to share what He has given me. Consistently using what God has given me, while cheerfully sharing it with others, is how I continue growing in my gift.

Chapter 7 - Discussion

Growing in my Gift

1. The author stays motivated to write because she knows that *someone* will be empowered by her work.

   Describe something you can do that you know helps other people.

2. God has always supplied the author with *everything* that she needs to do the work that He has given her to do. He even supplied her with confidence and motivation.

   Can you think of a time when God supplied something that you needed in order for you to help someone else?

An Urgent Call
To the Power of Ministry

Dr. Grace LaJoy Henderson

Chapter 8
The Call to Minister

As you can see by my life experiences, God placed a call to minister on my life at a very young age, and then He armed me with the *power* to walk in my ministry. He helped me to recognize the power that I had to empower others through Him. Then He placed me in a position to actually minister to others. While everyone is not called to be a full-time minister, everyone *is* called to minister the good news of Jesus Christ to others.

So, it is very important that we realize our ministry through our life experiences. If we do not, we can become frustrated with our circumstances because we do not understand them or why we are going through them. Realizing our "call to minister" is the exact same thing as "finding our purpose".

Walking in your "call to minister" means actively sharing the good news of Jesus Christ. Walking in your "call to minister" may also mean utilizing your *gift* in a way that brings others closer to God. But, before you can utilize your *gift*, you must know what it is. Please keep in mind that it is possible to have more than one *gift*. First, I am going to tell you the definition of *gift*. Second, I am going to give you some steps that you can take to recognize your *gift*. Then, I will teach you a little more about "the call to minister" and reveal the difference between a gift and a ministry.

The definition of *gift is an* unlearned skill that is given to us by God and is something that we do not have to go to school to learn. The fact that we do not have to do anything to get it is what makes it a gift. Here are some steps that you can take to recognize your *gift*:

Seek God about your gift. Ask God what He has given you to do for Him. Ask Him what your gift is and listen when he tells you.

Go in while the door is open. When God gives you something, take it at the very moment that He gives it to you. For example, if an idea for a book comes into your mind, write it down immediately. Do not say "I will write that book later" begin writing as soon as the idea comes to you, while you are still feeling the passion about it. Write it down while the idea is flowing; do not wait until the passion goes away and then try to write it without any passion.

Listen to the compliments that you receive from other people. Family members, teachers, friends, and church members sometimes detect your gift before you do. So, listen to what they have to say about you; and when you receive the same compliment from several people who do not know each other and who have not had communication with each other, that may be a sign of what your gift could be.

Know what you enjoy doing. Pay close attention to the things you do that are enjoyable for you. Ask yourself these two questions: If money was not an object, what would I spend my life doing? What makes me feel fulfilled and satisfied? Your answer to these questions may help you to pinpoint your natural gift.

Research the thing that you enjoy doing. There are several ways that you can learn more about the thing(s) that you enjoy doing: You can search the internet, take college courses, and talk to other people who have been successful at the thing that you enjoy.

Don't procrastinate. If God has given you something to do, do it. Take what little you have and do *something* with it. Do not wait until you can do more, but, use what God has already given you.

Start today. Do something *right now* with what God has given you. Then continue to do something every day with your gift. Remember that if you are spending a lot of time talking about it, then it is very likely that you are not doing it.

Note: The "gift" that I am referring to above is different from "spiritual" gifts. You can begin learning more about spiritual gifts by reading these sections of the Bible: Ephesians 4:11 and I Corinthians 12:7-10.

Now, let's learn more about "the call to minister" that God has placed on each of our lives. Sometimes, we search long and hard trying to figure out what our calling (or purpose) is. Well, now your search is over because I have good news for you: Your calling and purpose is *ministry*. Finding our calling and purpose is not as hard or mysterious as it sometimes seems. God has called and purposed each and every one of us to minister the good news of Jesus Christ and to share His Word with others. (Mark 16:15).

Contrary to popular belief, ministering is not the sole responsibility of pulpit preachers. We *all* are ministers. If we have become a part of God's family by accepting His forgiveness for our sins, through His Son Jesus Christ, then we are ministers and are required to share the good news of Jesus Christ with others.

Furthermore, sometimes we mistake our *gift* for our *ministry*. Here is the difference between the two: An example of one of my *gifts* is songwriting. It is a gift because I am usually asleep when songs come to me. When I hear a song in my sleep which includes the words, melody and the music, all I have to do is wake up and sing the song onto a tape recorder. I did not have to go to school or take any classes to learn how to write songs. I have never had to try to think about what to write for a song because songs are *given* to me. Therefore, my songwriting is a *gift*.

The word *ministry* has the exact same meaning as *calling* or *purpose*. They all mean "to share the good news of Jesus Christ". But, while *gift* is has a different meaning than *ministry*, the two can be combined for the purpose of ministry. For example, I can use my gift to write a book that shares the Word of God with those who read the book, and compel them to invite Jesus Christ into their lives. So, our gift and ministry play an important role in "the call to minister" that God has placed on each of our lives.

An Urgent Call　　　　　　　*Dr. Grace LaJoy Henderson*
To the Power of Ministry

Chapter 8 - Discussion

The Call to Minister

1. Walking in your "call to minister" means actively sharing the good news of Jesus Christ. It can also mean utilizing your gift in a way that brings others closer to God.

    Describe a time when you shared the good news of Jesus Christ with someone.

    Describe something you have done that caused someone else to grow closer to God.

2. One step that you can take to recognize your gift is to begin *now* by taking the little that you have and doing *something* with it.

    Describe something that you have, or something that you can do, that you feel is not good enough or big enough to share with others? Explain why you feel it is not good enough or big enough.

    What steps do you think you can take, starting today, to begin sharing what you have, or what you can do, with others?

3. True or False. God has called and purposed each and every one of us to share His Word with others.

4. True or False. Ministering is the sole responsibility of pulpit preachers.

Chapter 9
The Good News

We have talked a lot about the "good news" of Jesus Christ throughout this book. So, you may have questions like, Who is Jesus Christ? or What is the good news? Well, Jesus Christ is God's son. (John 3:16). The good news is that He was born, He died, and He rose from the dead for our sins so we can be forgiven and have everlasting life.

It all started with a young lady named Mary who was engaged to be married to a young man named Joseph. Mary was a virgin, but God caused her to become pregnant with a child without having sex. Joseph knew that Mary was a virgin and that he and Mary had not had sex. So, when he found out that she was pregnant, he was upset because he thought that she had cheated on him. The embarrassment Joseph endured caused him to want to call off the engagement. Then an angel of God spoke to Joseph in a dream and told him not to call off the engagement because Mary had not cheated and that she was still a virgin. The angel convinced Joseph that the power of the Holy Spirit caused Mary to become pregnant because she was going to give birth to Jesus, God's son. (Matthew 1:18-25).

Nine months later, through a turn of events, Jesus was born in a stable where horses lived. Then His mother wrapped Him in strips of cloth and laid Him in a manger, a bed made out of hay, to keep him warm. (Luke 2:7). People came to see the baby Jesus; to worship Him and bring Him gifts. (Matthew 2:11).

When Jesus was twelve years old, He knew that His purpose was to minister. (Luke 2:42,49). However, He did not have the *power* to actually begin working in ministry. He eventually received the power of the Holy Spirit. (Matthew 3:16)

When Jesus was about thirty years old, He began to work in His ministry. (Matthew 4:17). Throughout His ministry, He often performed miracles, including turning water into wine (John 2:7-9), healing sick people (John 5:8-9), causing blind people to see (John 9:6-7), and raising people from the dead (John 11:41-44), among many other things. He was able to perform these miracles because He had the power of God, also called the Holy Spirit, on Him. Some people accepted Jesus and some rejected Him. (John 1:11-12).

But, despite all of the people who rejected Him, Jesus continued to minister, telling people about God, His father. He called people to acknowledge God's power and to accept God in their hearts. He also told them that God loved them and could forgive them of their sins. Jesus had some special followers, called disciples, who believed everything that He taught them. (John 2:11).

Jesus knew that He was going to die so He prepared His disciples for that day. He told them not to worry because He would be back; that He was the way, the truth, and the life and that no man could come to God, His father, except through Him. (John 14:3-6). He encouraged His disciples to obey His teaching and told them that He would send the Holy Spirit to remind them of everything that He had taught them. He also told them that the Holy Spirit would give them comfort. (John 14:26).

When the day came for Jesus to die, He was beaten and nailed to a cross. (John 19:1-30). The men who killed Jesus were very mean to Him and showed Him no mercy before killing Him. But, even though they were treating Him terrible, Jesus said to God, as He hung on the cross before He died, "Father forgive them, because they do not understand what they are doing." (Luke 23:34).

After Jesus was dead, they took Him off of the cross and laid Him in a tomb. (John 19:38-42). But, three days later Jesus was no longer in the tomb because He had come back to life, just as He promised His disciples He would! (1 Corinthians 15:4). Jesus is still alive today! The best part of the good news is that we can experience God's forgiveness and have everlasting life through His son, Jesus Christ. (John 3:16).

An Urgent Call
To the Power of Ministry

Chapter 9 - Discussion

The Good News

1. The "good news of Jesus Christ" is the story of how Jesus was born, died, and rose from the dead for our sins so we can be forgiven by God and have everlasting life.

   Do you believe the good news of Jesus Christ?

   Please explain why you do, or don't, believe the good news of Jesus Christ.

2. Jesus began ministering full-time when he was about thirty years old. Even though some people rejected Him, He continued to tell them about the power of God.

   Describe a time when you were rejected, or someone was mean to you, after you told them about God.

3. Jesus told His disciples He would send the Holy Spirit to give them comfort and remind them of His teachings.

   Describe a time when you knew the Holy Spirit was giving you comfort or teaching you something.

4. True or False. Jesus is still alive today.

An Urgent Call
To the Power of Ministry

Dr. Grace LaJoy Henderson

Chapter 10
The Power of Ministry

When I look back to before I ever published my first book, I am reminded of the days when the church that I attended would bring in guest speakers who had also produced books and CDs. I would observe the guest speakers as they empowered the audience through their ministering messages. Then, when the message was finished, the speaker would advance to their book or CD table and sell to the long line of people who were waiting to purchase their products. Even though I had absolutely no idea that I would ever publish a book or produce a CD at that time, I would say to myself "I want that!" I wanted to be able to stand in front of an audience, empower, motivate, inspire, and minister to them; then have a long line of people at my table who were hungry to obtain my inspirational words of wisdom.

Although I had that desire, there were a few problems: I had not written a book; I did not know how to go about publishing and producing books and CDs; I did not know what real ministry was; I was *very* afraid and unwilling to speak in front of an audience; I was very shy overall. As I began to produce books, I found that all of the books were already written when it came time to publish them. For example after I got saved, I often became inspired to write poems at different times over a period of several years. So, when it came time to write the book, it was already written! I just needed to sort my poems into categories, format my book, design the book cover and publish the book. Many people have asked me how long it took to write my poetry book, but, what they do not realize is that I never *wrote* a *poetry book*...I wrote *poetry*, then I *published* my poetry in a book. I researched over a period of several years until I learned how to publish my book myself. I realized that the more I could do for myself, the less I would have to depend on others to do for me. So, I began taking steps towards publishing my book until eventually I came to a point where I had actually published my own book!

Every time I completed a book I was coming closer to my ministry, but I did not realize it because, for a long time, I thought the books *were* my ministry! After I had published several books, CDs and DVDs, God revealed to me that it was good that I had been obedient in writing, producing and publishing the books and other resources, but *that* was not my ministry. He revealed to me that true ministry is sharing the good news of Jesus Christ and preaching and teaching the Word of God. He revealed to me that my writing gift was only a *part* of, or a stepping stone to, my actual ministry. He revealed to me that the purpose of

An Urgent Call Dr. Grace LaJoy Henderson
To the Power of Ministry

the books and resources that I published was to finance the actual ministry. For example, when I share the good news of Jesus Christ with audiences, they will have the option of purchasing my books and resources so that they can continue to be empowered by my God-inspired words of wisdom even after I am gone from their presence.

Now that we understand the difference between a gift and true ministry, I want to talk about the *power* of ministry. The feelings of fear and rejection that I dealt with for most of my life, as a result of my mother leaving me, caused a sense of shyness inside of me. But, even though I still have that shyness, my confidence is now in God and knowing He has given me something to offer others. I understand that it is not about *me*, but it is all about *Him*. I realize now that I have something to say that empowers others, so there is no time for being shy anymore.

What do I have that other people need? I have four things: I have a personal relationship with God; I have knowledge about the good news of Jesus Christ; I have an understanding of the words in the Bible; and I have the Holy Spirit living on the inside of me. All of these things represent the *power* of ministry. All of these things are necessary in order to minister to others. The urgency comes from the fact that it is vital for us to begin walking in the *power* that we have to minister to others (1 Corinthians

9:16). If you can testify to having the four things that I have named above, then you have the *power* of ministry! It is important that you begin to *use* your power.

When you fully understand the urgent call to the power of ministry...

- ➢ You will know that God can do anything, at anytime, through anybody!
- ➢ You will know that *true* ministry is sharing the good news of Jesus Christ with others.
- ➢ You will know that teaching and preaching is not ministry unless we are teaching and preaching the Word of God...the Bible.
- ➢ You will know that merely working in a church auxiliary or religious organization is not ministry, but only a *part* of it; a very important part of it, however.
- ➢ You will know what your gifts are and use them in conjunction with your ministry.
- ➢ You will know that everything that you have gone through in life was to lead you to the point where you are able to minister to other people.
- ➢ You will know that what you are currently going through did not come to hurt you, but, to make you stronger, so that you may be equipped to minister to someone else as a result.

- You will know that your testimony is your story of how you accepted God, through Jesus Christ.
- You will understand that your life experiences are not your testimony, but, may be shared in conjunction with it.
- You will have the awareness that other people *need* your testimony, and you will understand the importance of sharing it.
- You will begin to actively share the power of God through the good news of Jesus Christ with other people.
- You will walk with great motivation, enthusiasm, and authority in *your* Urgent Call to the Power of Ministry!

An Urgent Call Dr. Grace LaJoy Henderson
To the Power of Ministry

Chapter 10 - Discussion

The Power of Ministry

1. At one time the author was afraid to speak to audiences and knew absolutely nothing about writing a book. However, she knew that she wanted to be a speaker and sell books after she observed other speakers do it.

   Describe a time when you observed someone else doing something and knew it was something that you would want to do.

2. God revealed to the author that *true* ministry is sharing the good news of Jesus Christ and preaching and teaching the Word of God.

   What are some ways you can exhibit true ministry?

3. There are four things that represent the "*power* of ministry": God, the good news of Jesus Christ, the Holy Spirit, and the Bible.

   What does the "power of ministry" mean to you?

   How can you apply the "power" to your life?

Closing

The Prayer of Salvation

I cannot end this book about *An Urgent Call to the Power of Ministry* without offering you the opportunity to accept God's forgiveness and invite Jesus Christ into your heart, if you have not already done so. God loves us so much that He allowed His son Jesus Christ to die for our sins so that we can have everlasting life. (John 3:16). We sin when we do not do what God tells us to do; and sin separates us from God. (Isaiah 59:2).

The Bible says that if you confess with your mouth the Lord Jesus and believe in your heart that God has raised Him from the dead, you will be saved! (Romans 10:9). You can ask Jesus Christ to come and live in your heart right now! If you desire forgiveness for your sins and would like to invite Jesus Christ to come into your life, then pray these words with me:

"Jesus, I confess that I am a sinner in need of salvation. I acknowledge You as Lord and I believe that You are God's son. Thank You for dying so that my sins can be forgiven. I believe that You are still alive today. Please come into my life and take full control of it. I accept Your forgiveness for my sin. Thank You for giving me eternal life and for the gift of the Holy Spirit. Amen"

If you prayed the prayer of salvation with me, accepting God's forgiveness through His Son Jesus Christ, you are now a part of the family of God! Your sins have been forgiven and you have eternal life with Christ. The Bible says anyone who belongs to Christ becomes a new person. The old life goes away and a new life begins. So, as time goes on, and you continue to follow Jesus Christ, your attitudes and actions will begin to change. (2 Corinthians 5:17).

If you prayed the prayer of salvation with me, then there are *three* things that you need: A Bible, a prayer partner, and a church home. *A Bible* is God's Word and it is the primary way that He speaks to us. (John 1:1). *A prayer partner* is important because prayer is the primary way that we speak to God. When two or more people pray together God is with them. (Matthew 18:20). *A church home* is important because God instructs us to be around other believers, which is a great way to continue to grow in our faith in God. (Hebrews 10:25).

If you prayed the prayer of salvation with me, you now have a testimony to share with others and you are now equipped to begin walking, with confidence, in the *power* of ministry!

Recommended Books and Resources

The Purpose Driven Life *by* Rick Warren

The Purpose Driven Church *by* Rick Warren

The Prayer of Jabez *by* Bruce Wilkinson

Rich Dad, Poor Dad *by* Robert T. Kiyosaki

The Shack *by* William P. Young

Passion for Your Purpose *by* Gloria Thomas-Anderson

God's Purpose for Your Life *by* Barbara Wentrobel

Rise to Your Destiny Woman of God *by* Barbara Wentrobel

Simple Church *by* Thom S. Rainer

Your Best Life Now *by* Joel Osteen

Living the Life You Were Meant to Live *by* Tom Paterson

An Urgent Call
To the Power of Ministry 　　　　*Dr. Grace LaJoy Henderson*

Glossary of Terms

Auxiliary – An area of the church or religious organization in which one can work. Working in an auxiliary does not, in itself, constitute ministry, but is an important part of ministry.

Call – An unction from God to do something.

Calling – God's instruction to us to teach others about the "power" which is only found in these things: God, the Holy Bible, and the good news of Jesus Christ.

Gift – Something that God gives us to do for him. An unlearned talent given to us by God; something that we do not need formal education to learn.

God's Word – The words that are written in the Holy Bible.

Gospel – The good news of Jesus Christ.

Holy Bible – A book that contains words that have been inspired by God. Also known as God's Word.

Jesus Christ – The Son of God.

Life experience – Things that happen to us, through us, in us, and for us, during the course of our lives.

Ministry – Introducing, sharing, preaching, and/or teaching others about God's Word, including the good news of Jesus Christ.

Power – God, the Holy Spirit, the Holy Bible, the good news of Jesus Christ.

Preach – Often and consistently sharing the Bible, including the good news of Jesus Christ, with others.

Purpose – God's plan, or His intention, for us to share, with others, the good news of Jesus Christ.

Salvation – God's forgiveness and eternal life with God through accepting Jesus Christ into our lives.

Sin – To not do what God tells us to do.

Teach – To share the Bible, including the good news of Jesus Christ with others.

Testimony – The story of how we came to accept God's forgiveness and the good news of Jesus Christ.

Urgent – Vital, important, necessary. We must understand, and act on, something that is "urgent" or else there could be negative consequences.

Index

Auxiliary 3,82,93
Bible 3,4,6,10,42,43,47,67,81,82,87,88,93,94
Call 1,2,4,6,10,65,66,67,93
Calling 10,68,67,69,82,87,93
Gift(s) 14,23-26,30,31,34,47-51,57-59,62, 65-68,68,69,80,81,82,87
God's Word 88,93
Good News 2-5,9,10,37,38,43,65,68,69,73,75,80-83,93,94
Jesus Christ 2-6,9,10,37,38,42,43,65,68,69,73,75, 80-83,87,88,93,94
Life experience 4-6,10,65,83,93
Ministry 1-6,9,10,20,29,47,50,58,65,66,68,69,74,79, 80-83,87,88,93
Power 1-4,6,9,29,37,38,41,42,53,65,74,79,81-83,87, 88,93
Preach(ing) 3,80,82,94
Purpose 5,8-10,20,48,65,68,69,80,94
Salvation 3,87,88,94
Sin 5,39,47,87,94
Teach 3,42,80,82,93,94
Testimony 3-6,10,37,42,47,83,88,94
Urgent 1,2,4,6,9,82,83,87,94

Books and Resources Available by Dr. Grace LaJoy Henderson

Sexual Purity and the Young Woman: A Guide to Sexual Purity (Book)

Writer's Breakthrough: *Steps To Copyright and Publish Your Own Book*
(Book and CD)

More Than Mere Words: *Poetry That Ministers*
(Christian Poetry Book)

Understanding Each Other: *A Guide for Parents and their Children* (Book)

In My Mama's House
(Book – ages 13-18)

How Can Jesus Be God?
(Children's Book)

Poetic Book Series
Diversity in our Schools, Diversity in our Workplace
The Bad Butt Kids, He's Worth It, Our Employees…Our Cornerstones

Poetic Empowerment
(Spoken Word CD)

Songs by Grace LaJoy
(Gospel Music CD)

The Life of Grace LaJoy
(DVD)

To learn more please visit us online at
www.gracelajoy.com or www.writersbreakthrough.com

An Urgent Call   *Dr. Grace LaJoy Henderson*
To the Power of Ministry

TO THE *POWER* *of* MINISTRY

An Urgent Call
To the Power of Ministry

Dr. Grace LaJoy Henderson

URGENT CALL
TO THE *POWER* *of* MINISTRY

www.ingramcontent.com/pod-product-compliance
Lightning Source LLC
Chambersburg PA
CBHW051455290426
44109CB00016B/1762